Cat Breeds

SCOTTISH FOLDS

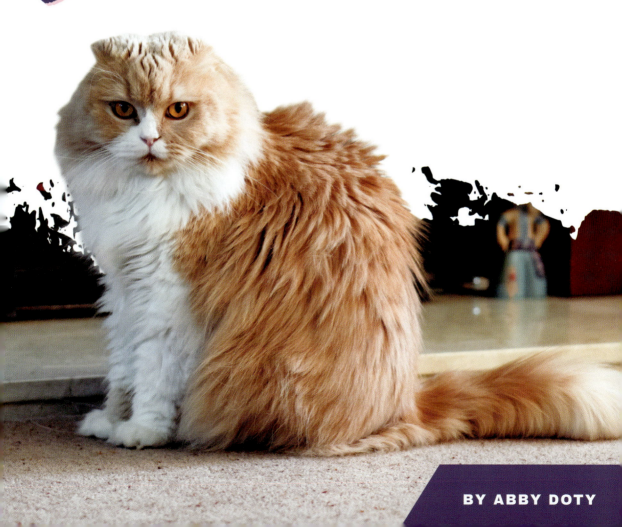

BY ABBY DOTY

WWW.APEXEDITIONS.COM

Copyright © 2025 by Apex Editions, Mendota Heights, MN 55120. All rights reserved. No part of this book may be reproduced or utilized in any form or by any means without written permission from the publisher.

Apex is distributed by North Star Editions:
sales@northstareditions.com | 888-417-0195

Produced for Apex by Red Line Editorial.

Photographs ©: Shutterstock Images, cover, 1, 4–5, 7, 8–9, 10–11, 12–13, 14, 15, 16–17, 18, 19, 20–21, 22–23, 24–25, 26, 27, 29

Library of Congress Control Number: 2024944180

ISBN
979-8-89250-314-3 (hardcover)
979-8-89250-352-5 (paperback)
979-8-89250-427-0 (ebook pdf)
979-8-89250-390-7 (hosted ebook)

Printed in the United States of America
Mankato, MN
012025

NOTE TO PARENTS AND EDUCATORS

Apex books are designed to build literacy skills in striving readers. Exciting, high-interest content attracts and holds readers' attention. The text is carefully leveled to allow students to achieve success quickly. Additional features, such as bolded glossary words for difficult terms, help build comprehension.

TABLE OF CONTENTS

CHAPTER 1
BUSY CATS 4

CHAPTER 2
BREED HISTORY 10

CHAPTER 3
CUTE AND CUDDLY 16

CHAPTER 4
CAT CARE 22

COMPREHENSION QUESTIONS • 28
GLOSSARY • 30
TO LEARN MORE • 31
ABOUT THE AUTHOR • 31
INDEX • 32

CHAPTER 1

BUSY CATS

A Scottish fold sits on a couch. She cuddles with her owner. Then, the cat hops down to the floor. She creeps up to her brother and jumps on him.

Scottish folds prefer a mix of snuggling and active play each day.

The cat and her brother run through the house. They **wrestle** each other and play with toys. They also climb up a cat tree.

FAST FACT

Scottish folds tend to get along with children and with other pets.

Scottish folds use cat trees to hide, play, or view rooms from up high.

While the cats play, their owner hides several treats. Soon, the cats begin their search. They look beneath tables and behind chairs. They find all the treats.

MIND GAMES

Scottish folds are smart cats. They get bored easily. Toys and games can help them stay entertained. So can food puzzles. Cats must get food out of a **container**.

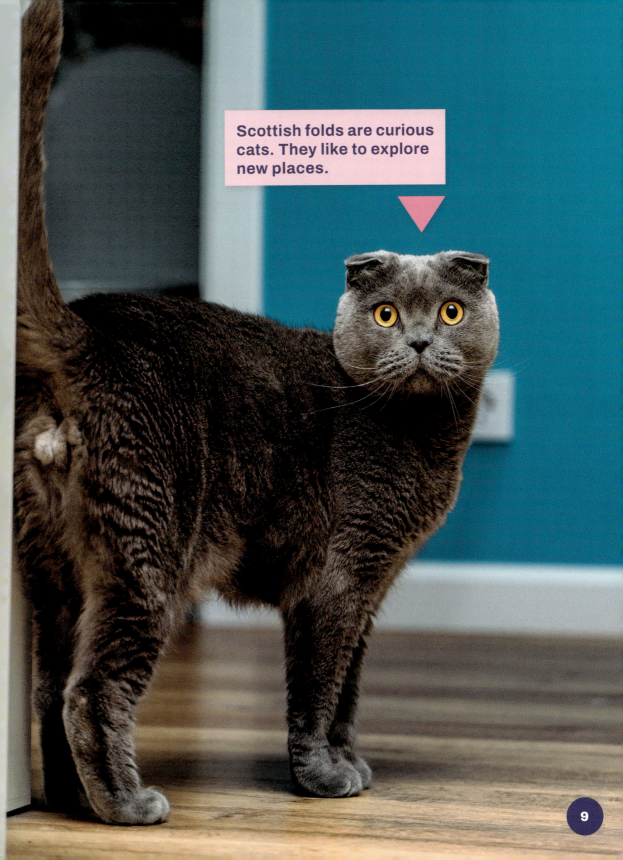

Scottish folds are curious cats. They like to explore new places.

CHAPTER 2

BREED HISTORY

In the 1960s, a man named William Ross saw a cat living on a nearby farm in Scotland. Her name was Susie. Susie and some of her kittens had folded ears.

Scotland is in the northern part of the United Kingdom.

Susie's owner gave one of her kittens to Ross. Then Ross had the folded-eared cat **mate** with other cats. This began the Scottish fold **breed**.

Some kittens' ears fold after a few weeks. Others stay straight.

FAST FACT
About half of all Scottish fold kittens get folded ears.

In 2023, Scottish folds were one of the most common cat breeds.

Scottish folds spread to other countries. They became popular in many places. However, the cats often have health problems. So, some people think owning them is wrong.

HEALTH PROBLEMS

A **gene** gives Scottish folds their bent ears. This gene affects other body parts, too. It weakens bones and **joints**. Many Scottish folds feel pain or stiffness.

Some Scottish folds can't run or jump because of joint problems.

CHAPTER 3

CUTE AND CUDDLY

Scottish folds are medium-sized cats. Most weigh between 6 and 13 pounds (3 and 6 kg). The cats have short necks and round faces.

Scottish folds have large, round eyes.

The gene that causes folded ears can also make a cat's legs and tail stiff.

All Scottish folds have small ears. Many have ears that fold forward. The cats also have short legs and tails. Their thick fur comes in many colors.

FAST FACT
Many Scottish folds have short fur. But some have long coats.

Scottish folds with long hair are often called Highland folds.

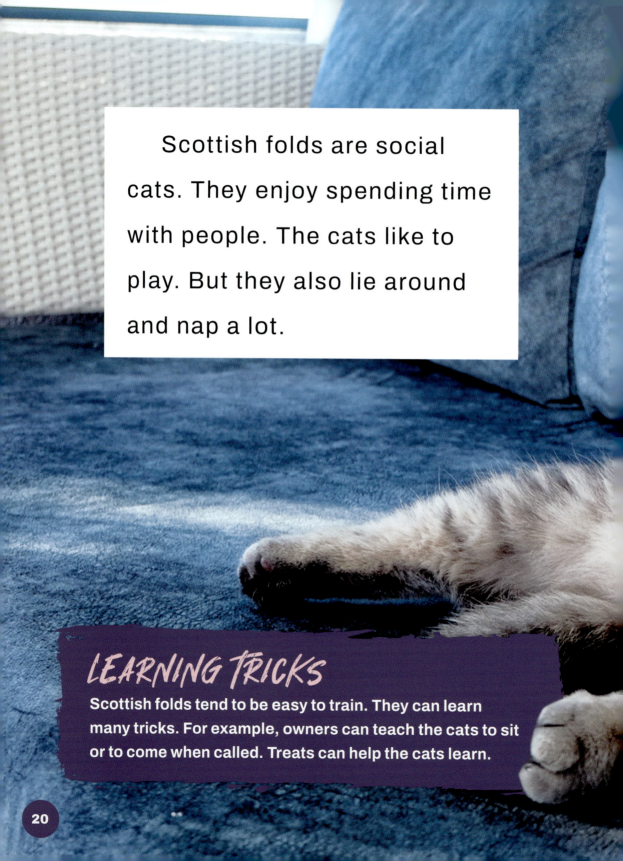

Scottish folds are social cats. They enjoy spending time with people. The cats like to play. But they also lie around and nap a lot.

LEARNING TRICKS

Scottish folds tend to be easy to train. They can learn many tricks. For example, owners can teach the cats to sit or to come when called. Treats can help the cats learn.

Scottish folds often sit with their legs spread in front of them.

CHAPTER 4

CAT CARE

Short-haired Scottish folds need to be brushed once or twice a week. Long-haired cats may need more grooming. Some must be brushed four times a week.

Brushing can get rid of tangles and loose hairs.

Scottish folds can gain weight easily. So, exercise is important. Owners should spend time playing with their cats each day.

FAST FACT
Scottish folds need about 15 minutes of exercise per day.

◀ **A Scottish fold may start to feel more joint pain if it does not move around enough.**

Scottish folds with joint pain may not want to be held or petted.

Owners should watch for signs of health problems, too. Sick cats may not play as often. Or they may act more **aggressive**. These cats may need to visit the vet.

EAR ISSUES

Folded ears trap dirt and **germs**. So, they are at risk for **infections**. Owners should check their cats' ears each week. They should clean out dirt and wax.

Owners can use wet cloths or cotton balls to clean their Scottish folds' ears.

COMPREHENSION QUESTIONS

Write your answers on a separate piece of paper.

1. Write a few sentences explaining the main ideas of Chapter 4.

2. Do you think people should keep breeding Scottish folds? Why or why not?

3. What was the name of the first cat with folded ears?
    - A. William
    - B. Susie
    - C. Ross

4. Why might sick cats not play as often?
    - A. Sick cats might feel pain when they move.
    - B. Sick cats might feel more active than usual.
    - C. Sick cats might feel very hungry.

5. What does **popular** mean in this book?

Scottish folds spread to other countries. They became popular in many places.

    A. no longer living
    B. found in just one place
    C. common in many areas

6. What does **grooming** mean in this book?

Short-haired Scottish folds need to be brushed once or twice a week. Long-haired cats may need more grooming. Some must be brushed four times a week.

    A. cleaning and caring for fur
    B. petting fur
    C. tangling and messing up fur

Answer key on page 32.

GLOSSARY

aggressive
Strong and quick to attack.

breed
A specific type of cat that has its own look and abilities.

container
An object, such as a box or jar, that can hold other things.

gene
A tiny part of a cell that controls how an animal looks.

germs
Tiny living things that can cause sickness.

infections
Sicknesses caused by germs.

joints
Parts of the body that connect two bones and allow for movement.

mate
To form a pair and come together to have babies.

wrestle
To fight with or grab at another animal.

TO LEARN MORE

BOOKS

Jaycox, Jaclyn. *Read All About Cats*. North Mankato, MN: Capstone Publishing, 2021.

Klukow, Mary Ellen. *Scottish Folds*. Mankato, MN: Amicus, 2020.

Pearson, Marie. *Cat Behavior*. Minneapolis: Abdo Publishing, 2024.

ONLINE RESOURCES

Visit **www.apexeditions.com** to find links and resources related to this title.

ABOUT THE AUTHOR

Abby Doty is a writer, editor, and booklover from Minnesota.

INDEX

B
breeds, 12

E
ears, 10, 12–13, 15, 18, 27
exercise, 25

F
fur, 18–19

G
grooming, 22

H
health, 14–15, 26

O
owner, 4, 8, 12, 20, 25–27

P
play, 6, 8, 20, 25–26

R
Ross, William, 10, 12

S
Scotland, 10
smart, 8
social, 20
Susie, 10, 12

T
toys, 6, 8

ANSWER KEY:
1. Answers will vary; 2. Answers will vary; 3. B; 4. A; 5. C; 6. A